Keen Kutter

An Illustrated Value Guide

By Jerry and Elaine Heuring

COLLECTOR BOOKS
P. O. Box 3009
Paducah, KY 42001

The current values in this book should be used only as a guide. They are not intended to set prices, which vary from one section of the country to another. Auction prices as well as dealer prices vary greatly and are affected by conditions as well as demand. Neither the Authors nor the Publisher assumes responsibility for any losses that might be incurred as a result of consulting this guide.

Additional copies of this book may be ordered from:

COLLECTOR BOOKS
P. O. Box 3009
Paducah, Kentucky 42001

@ $5.95 Add $1.00 for postage and handling.

Copyright: Jerry and Elaine Heuring, 1984
ISBN: 0-89145-246-X

Printed by IMAGE GRAPHICS, Paducah, Kentucky

Dedication

To Wendy Michelle
Our Lovely Daughter

Acknowledgements

Our very special thanks to Alan Reiman, our photographer, for the excellent job he performed in laying out and capturing the logo details.

Our very special thanks to Richard Young, our photograph developer, for his patience and excellent job in bringing out the detail work in the photographs.

Our very special love to our daughter, Wendy, for the many times she willingly went with us to auctions, flea markets, shops, and antique shows. Over the years she has developed an eye for the Keen Kutter name or logo.

Our special appreciation to our family and friends who kept Wendy on the many weekends she wasn't able to go with us.

A final thanks to our friends who encouraged us to write this value guide. It was something we dreamed of doing for years. Through our friends' encouragement, this dream has come true.

Table of Contents

Introduction

All illustrations in this value guide are from our personal collection, a collection which got its start in 1976 at an antiques show. Until that time, we had nothing in particular that we collected. At that show, we spotted a Keen Kutter hatchet and the emblem/logo fascinated us. So . . . we purchased the hatchet and decided to start a collection of Keen Kutter tools. Over the years, visiting various antiques shops, flea markets, and shows, we were discovering Keen Kutter products other than tools. With prices being more affordable back then, before we knew it, we had expanded to kitchen items, cutlery, advertising items, and even a hand fan. In the seven short years we have been collecting, we have accumulated approximately six hundred different pieces!

This Keen Kutter value guide illustrates only a small portion of our vast collection. Every item in this guide, as well as in our collection, is marked "Keen Kutter" either with the name written out or in logo form.

The condition of ANY item is critical in determining its value. If the name or logo is battered or unreadable, the value is considerably less than it would be for an item in mint condition. For example, if you have a hammer with the logo in good condition, you have a hammer worth about $20. But, if that logo is scratched or unreadable, it is worth only about $5 or less.

All the items in our collection are in "very good" to "mint" condition. As any serious collector, we upgrade items at every available opportunity, thus increasing the overall value of the entire collection..

We have found our varied collection of tools, lawn and garden and household items to be very interesting and enjoyable . . . a hobby the whole family shares. A close examination of the Keen Kutter products tells us why Shapleigh Hardware Company adapted their guarantee and slogan. These tools and products were indeed "top of the line" products.

History

Augustus Frederick Shapleigh was born in 1810. He was employed in a retail hardware store at the age of 14. Edward Campbell Simmons was born in 1839 and was employed in a wholesale hardware store at the age of 17. The story of the achievements of these two hardware clerks reads like a romance.

Young Shapleigh, as junior partner of Rogers Brothers & Company, wholesale hardware dealers in Philadelphia, brought to St. Louis, in 1843, a sufficient stock to open a branch of that company under the name of Rogers, Shapleigh & Company.

In 1847, the firm became Shapleigh, Day & Company, continuing until 1863, when Mr. Day retired and the firm became A. F. Shapleigh & Company.

Mr. Simmons' parents moved to St. Louis in 1846 when he was a lad of seven. At 17, he was employed by Child Pratt & Company, wholesale hardware dealers. In 1859, he went to work for Wilson, Levering & Waters. He became a partner in that firm six years later and in 1869, after the death and retirement of other members of the firm, he reorganized as E. C. Simmons & Company.

In 1864, the Shapleigh firm adapted DIAMOND EDGE as the brand name for a line of superior tools and cutlery which immediately became popular with the trade they served. In 1870, the Simmons firm chose KEEN KUT-TER as the brand name for their line of high grade tools and cutlery. As there were no laws whereby these brands could be trademarked, both firms were compelled to await the action of Congress before application for registration could be filed.

Shapleigh's first catalog, a small paperback price book containing no illustrations, was issued in 1853. By 1880, both firms published large, well-bound, general line catalogs, which, with the sole exception of one issued by Markley, Alling, & Company of Chicago, were the first of this type to make their appearance in the hardware trade of the United States.

Prosperous years followed for both firms; their trade areas steadily expanded and eventually the combined sales of the two companies attained so large a volume as to firmly establish St. Louis as the largest distributor of hardware in the nation.

In 1898, Mr. Simmons retired, as did Mr. Shapleigh in 1901, both having the satisfaction of seeing the businesses they had built carried on with constantly increasing strength and influence. The death of Mr. Shapleigh came in 1902, that of Mr. Simmons in 1920.

As the result of negotiations in the spring of 1940, Shapleigh Hardware Company purchased, for cash, all assets of Simmons Hardware Company, effective July 1, 1940. Proceeds of the sale were distributed to stockholders of the latter company, whose charter was surrendered in due time.

Upon purchase, Shapleigh Hardware Company occupied all of the buildings used by Simmons Hardware Company at Ninth and Spruce Streets, as well as additional warehouse facilities found available, in St. Louis. A majority of the Simmons' personnel became associated with Shapleigh's. All Simmons' trademarked lines were continued and the business, thus greatly enlarged, operated smoothly and successfully under Shapleigh's management until closing in the early 1950s.

This trademark was adopted by Simmons Hardware Company in 1870. It was first applied to high grade axes; but the favor with which they were received by the trade encouraged the immediate development of an extensive line of Keen Kutter tools and cutlery.

The long standing Keen Kutter guarantee was: "We guarantee this tool to be properly made and tempered, and that the steel is free from manufacturing defects. If found otherwise and returned to us we will give a new one for it." Keen Kutter's slogan was: "The Recollection of QUALITY Remains Long after the PRICE is Forgotten."

Tools

Oak wall tool cabinet, 27½″ high, 19″ wide, 8″ deep. Cabinet, $200.00. Price WITH tools would vary based on types of tool, condition, quantities, etc.

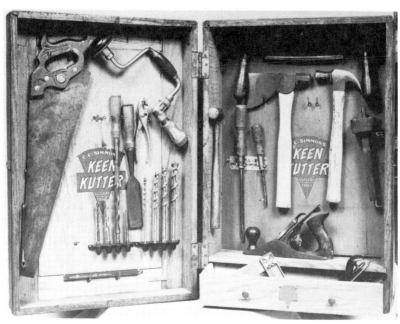

Oak cabinet complete with tools.

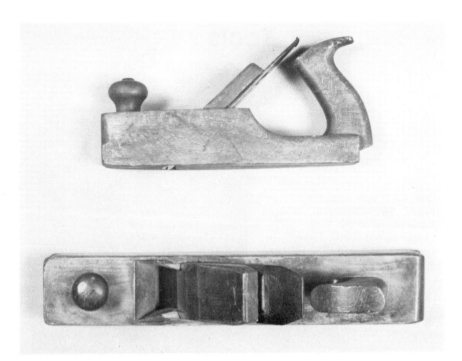

These two wood planes are unique due to their unique logo, as shown on the blade of the bottom one. This was probably Keen Kutter's first logo. It is half-moon shaped with saw-tooth design. These logos are found on the front wood base part of the plane as well as on the blade. $25.00-$35.00.

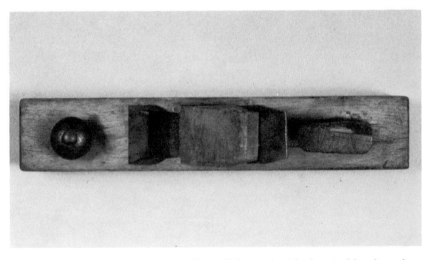

15″ Wood running plane. "Keen Kutter" is marked in front of knob and on blade. $18.00-$25.00.

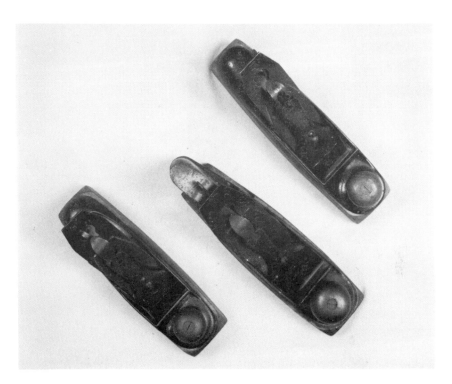

TOP: 9″ No. K23 wood bottom plane. MIDDLE: 9½″ No. K35 wood bottom plane with smooth wood handle. BOTTOM: 8″ No. K22 wood bottom plane. $18.00-$30.00 each.

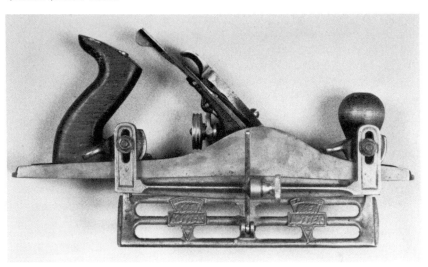

No. 5 jack plane, smooth bottom with jointer or plane gauge attachment, adjustable angles between 30° and 90°. Plane, $20.00-$35.00; Attachment, $45.00-$65.00.

Iron bench planes. LEFT: No. 4 smooth bottom plane with logo on blade and lever cap, $25.00-$35.00. CENTER: 14″ No. 5 smooth bottom jack plane with logo on blade and lever cap, $20.00-$35.00. RIGHT: 9″ No. 4 corrugated bottom, has words "Keen Kutter" written out on lever cap, $25.00-$40.00.

Iron bench planes. TOP: 24″ No. K8 smooth bottom, $35.00-$45.00. CENTER: 22″ No. KK7 corrugated bottom, $35.00-$55.00. BOTTOM LEFT: 14″ No. K5 corrugated bottom, $25.00-$35.00. BOTTOM RIGHT: 9″ No. K3 corrugated bottom, $50.00-$65.00.

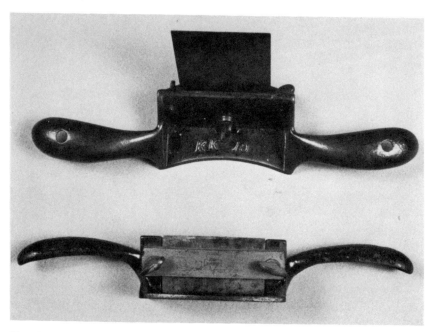

Handled cabinet scrapers. Top is a No. KK79 and the bottom is a No. K79.
$25.00-$35.00 each.

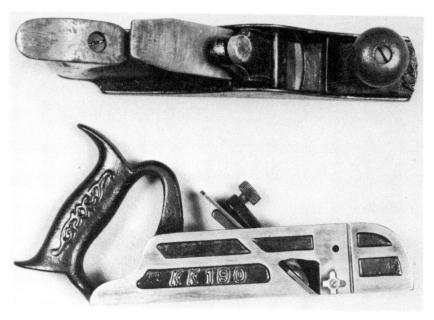

TOP: 9½″ No. K240 scrub plane, $45.00-$60.00. BOTTOM: 8″ No. KK190 rabbet plane, $45.00-$55.00.

Iron block planes. TOP ROW, LEFT TO RIGHT: 5-3/8″ No. KK103 adjustable, $15.00-$20.00. 7″ No. KK110 non-adjustable; 7″ No. K110 non-adjustable; and 7″ non-adjustable without KK number-marking on blade alone, $15.00-$20.00 each. BOTTOM ROW, LEFT TO RIGHT: 7½″ No. KK130 non-adjustable double cutter (one for block plane, one for bullnose), $35.00-$45.00. 7″ No. K220 adjustable with old style cap; 7″ No. K220 adjustable with lever type cap; 7″ non-adjustable marked on blade alone, $15.00-$20.00 each.

TOP: 8″ Screw wrench with wood knife handle, has "Black Jack" under the logo, $20.00-$30.00. BOTTOM: Screw wrench, 12″, with metal handle, has "Black Jack" under the logo, $20.00-$30.00.

TOP: No. K2 pipe cutter three-wheel pattern from ½″ to 2″ capacity, $35.00.
BOTTOM: No. KP200 pipe vise 1/8″ to 2″ capacity, $35.00.

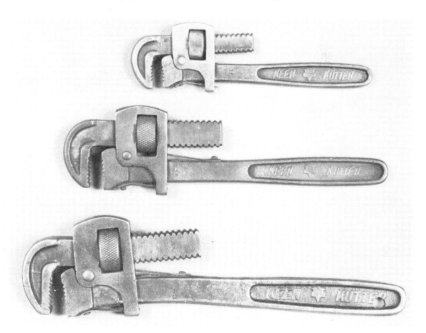

Pipe wrenches, sizes 8″, 10″, and 12″, $15.00-$25.00.

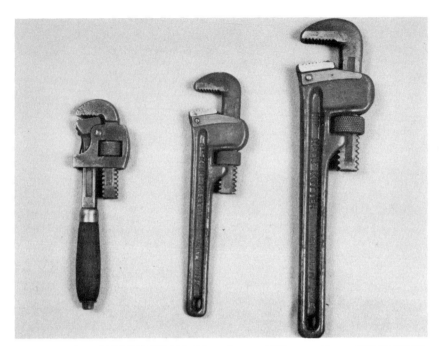

Pipe wrenches. LEFT TO RIGHT: 8″ made on a Stillson pattern, $20.00-30.00. 8″, $15.00-25.00. 10″, $15.00-25.00.

LEFT TO RIGHT: 6″ Adjustable wrench; 8″ chromium adjustable wrench; 8″ black steel adjustable wrench, $15.00-$20.00 each. Open end wrench, $15.00.

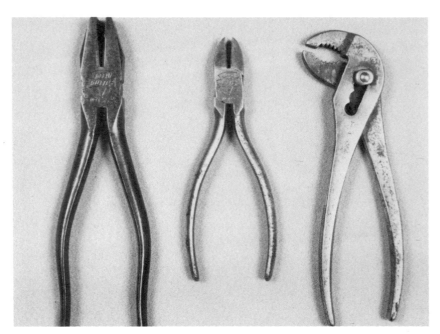

LEFT: Electrician or lineman pliers. CENTER: Diagonal cutting pliers. RIGHT: 75° combination slip joint pliers. $18.00-$25.00 each.

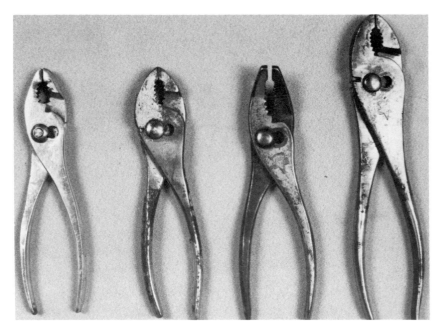

LEFT TO RIGHT: Slip joint pliers; slip joint pliers with screw driver on handle; thin narrow 30° bent nose slip joint pliers; 7" slip joint pliers with screw driver on handle. $12.00-$20.00 each.

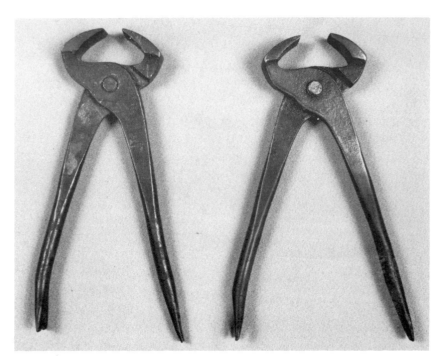

Carpenter pinchers, $10.00 each.

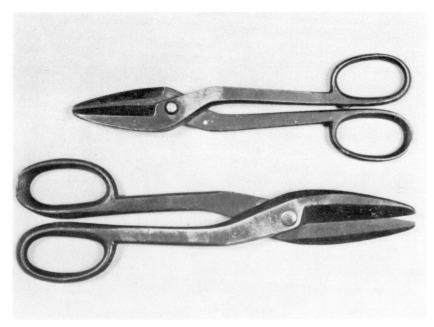

Tinners snips, $15.00-$20.00 each.

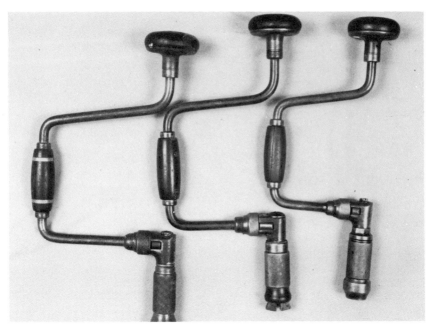

14″ Sweep No. KA14; 12″ sweep No. KA12; 10″ sweep No. KA10.
$20.00-$30.00 each.

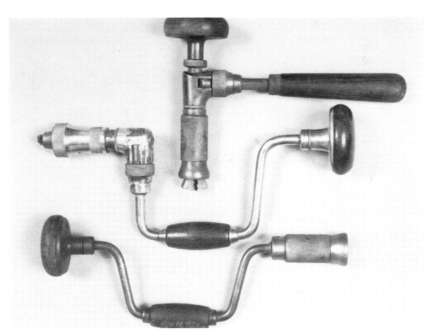

Bit braces. TOP: Hand-held ratchet brace, $45.00. CENTER: 8″ Sweep No.
K18, $20.00-$30.00. BOTTOM: 6″ Sweep No. KA6, $25.00-$35.00.

Auger bit set in roll-up case, set of seven from ¼″ to 1″, $35.00-$40.00.

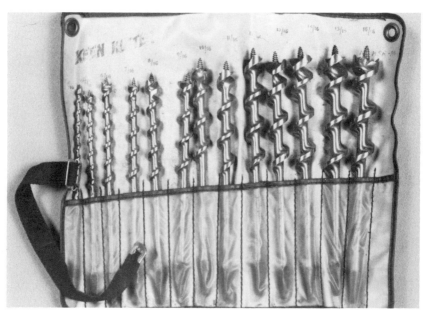

Auger bit set in roll-up case, set of 13 from ¼″ to 1″, $40.00-$45.00.

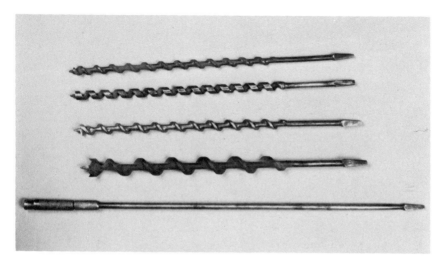

TOP: 9/16″ Car bit, 17″ long. 2ND: ½″ Ship auger car bit, 16½″ long. 3RD: 11/16″ Car bit, 17″ long. 4th: 1-1/16″ Car bit, 17″ long. $3.00-$6.00 each. BOTTOM: 24″ Bit extension, $15.00.

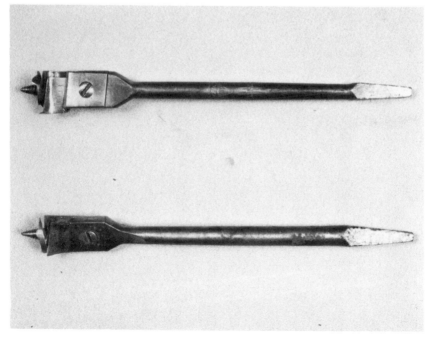

Expansion bits, one with logo and patent 3/12/13; other just has "Keen Kutter" on it, $10.00-$15.00.

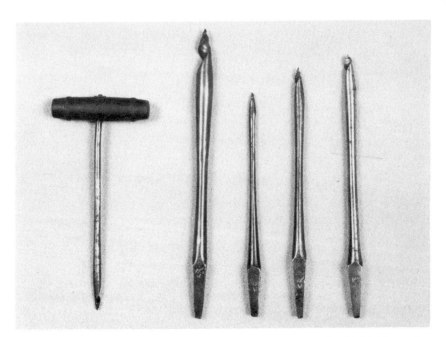

Gimlet, $6.00-$8.00. Gimlet bits (four different sizes), $1.00-$3.00 each.

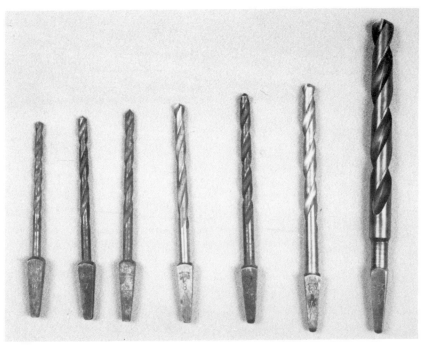

Brace drill bits, $1.00-$3.00 each.

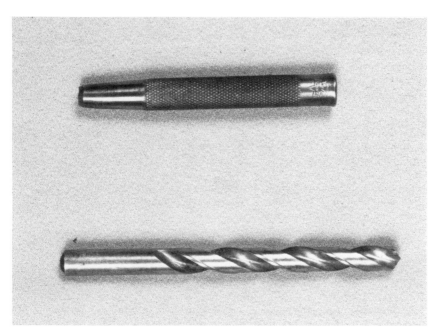

Leather punch, $8.00. Twist drill bit, $3.00.

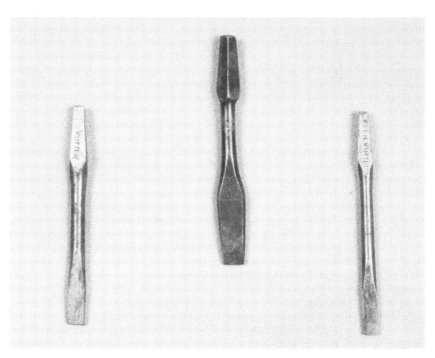

Brace screw driver bits, $1.00-$3.00 each.

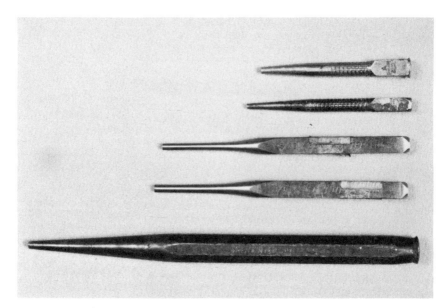

TOP TO BOTTOM: 5/32" Nail set, $6.00-$10.00. 3/32" Nail set, $6.00-$10.00. 5/32" Machine punch, $8.00-$12.00. 3/16" Machine punch, $8.00-$12.00. Straight tapered machine punch, $8.00-$12.00.

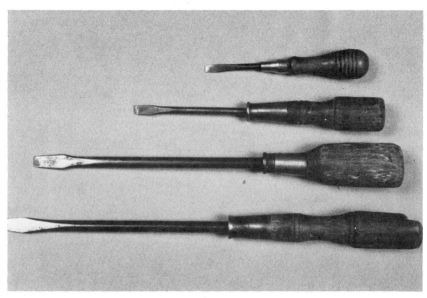

Screwdrivers, $12.00-$25.00 each.

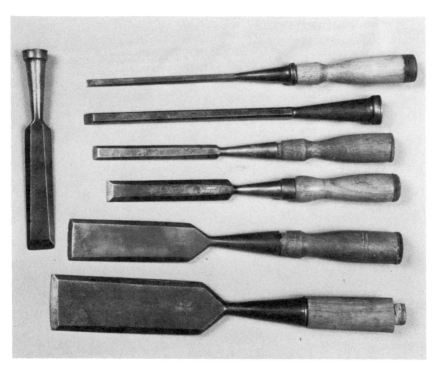

Socket firmer chisels, $8.00-$15.00.

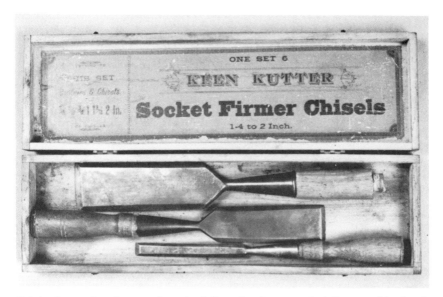

Original wooden box and part of the six-piece socket firmer chisel set, $30.00-$40.00. Box without chisels, $15.00.

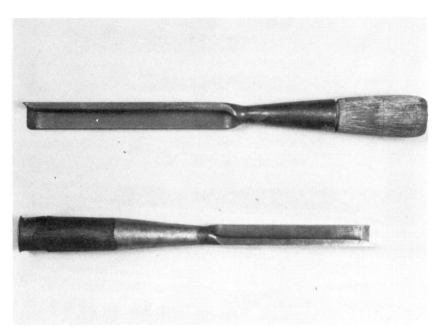

Corner wood chisels, sizes ¾″ and 7/8″, $15.00-$20.00 each.

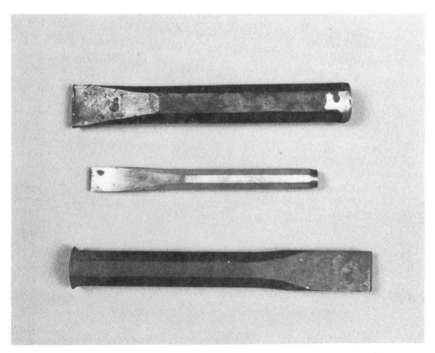

Cold chisels, sizes 1-1/8″, 5/8″, and 1″, $8.00-$12.00 each.

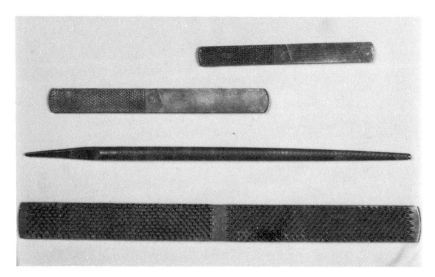

TOP TO BOTTOM: 8″ shoe rasp; 10″ shoe rasp; 14″ round file; 18″ rasp, $7.00-$12.00 each.

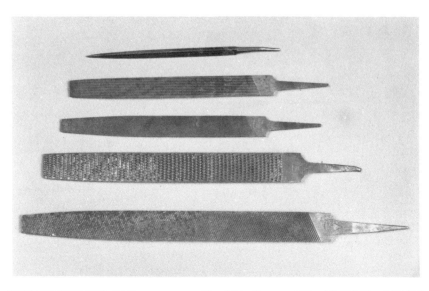

TOP TO BOTTOM: 6″ three-square file; 8″ half-round file; 8″ flat file; 10″ flat wood rasp; 12″ half-round file, $7.00-$12.00 each.

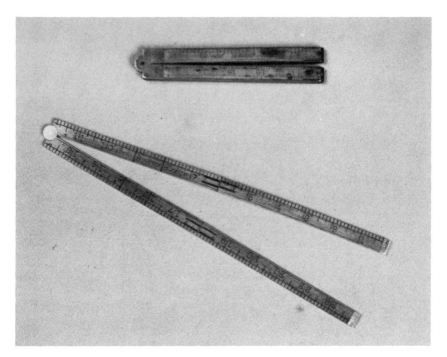

TOP: No. K620 brass bound 2' fold-up rule, $15.00-$20.00. BOTTOM: No. K680 wooden 2' fold-up rule, $12.00-$20.00.

Framing squares. TOP: No. KC3 16" tongue, copper finish. BOTTOM: No. K3 17" tongue. $20.00 each.

TOP: Sliding T-bevel square with cast iron handle, 9¾" blade, $25.00-$35.00. CENTER: Sliding T-bevel square, wood handle, 8" blade, logo marked on blade, $20.00. BOTTOM: Sliding T-bevel square with 8" blade, cast iron handle, $25.00-$35.00.

Tri-squares. TOP: 7½", logo on blade, $15.00-$20.00. CENTER: 7¼", nickel plated cast iron handle with "Keen Kutter" on it, $25.00. BOTTOM: 4½", logo on blade, $15.00-$20.00.

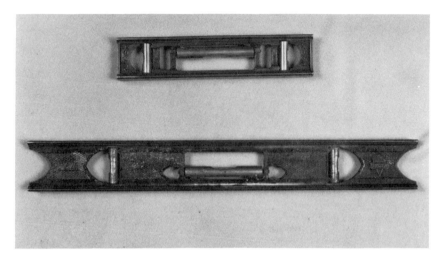

TOP: No. K69 9″ cast iron level, $65.00-$75.00. BOTTOM: No. K618 18″ cast iron level, $75.00-$100.00.

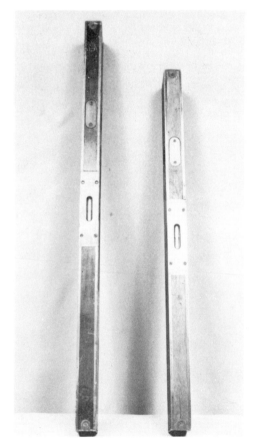

LEFT: No. KK40 30″ level, brass bound, adjustable, with brass side view (mint condition), $75.00-$100.00. RIGHT: No. KK50 26″ level, brass bound, adjustable, $65.00-$85.00.

24″, 26″, 28″ and 30″ No. KK0 levels, $20.00-$30.00 each.

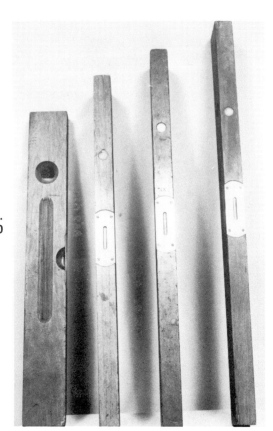

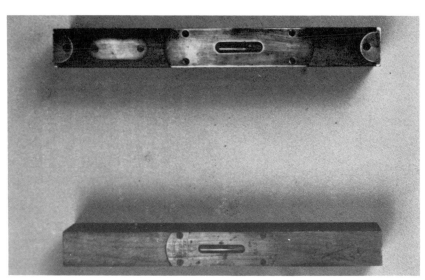

TOP: No. KK3 12″ level, adjustable with brass ends, $40.00-$50.00.
BOTTOM: No. KK13 12″ level, non-adjustable, mint condition, $40.00-$50.00.

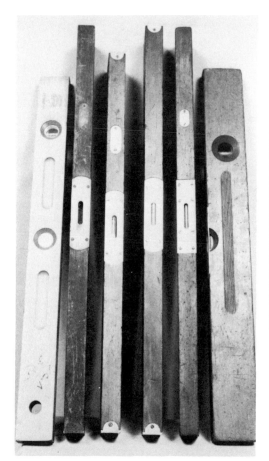

LEFT TO RIGHT: Shapleigh Keen Kutter No. F3755GK 28″ non-adjustable level, mint condition, $30.00. No. KK3 level, 30″ brass ends, adjustable, $30.00-$35.00. No. KK3 level, 28″ brass ends, $30.00-$35.00. No. KK30 level, 30″ brass adjustable duplex side views with brass ends, $40.00-$50.00. No. KK2 30″ adjustable level, $20.00-$30.00. No. KK2 28″ non-adjustable level, $20.00-$30.00.

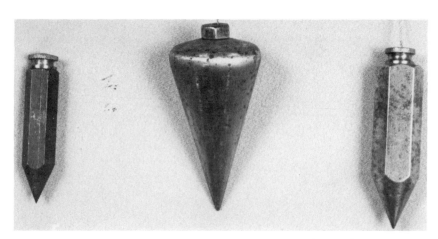

Plumb bob. LEFT: 6 oz. hexagon, steel, $12.00-$20.00. CENTER: 16 oz. round with screw top, $12.00-$20.00. RIGHT: 12 oz. hexagon, steel, $12.00-$20.00.

Hammers. LEFT: 20 oz. curved claw, round neck, $15.00-$25.00.
CENTER: 7 oz. No. KA7 round neck, curved claw, $40.00. RIGHT: 16
oz. No. KD11½ dynamic curved claw with round neck, $15.00-$25.00.

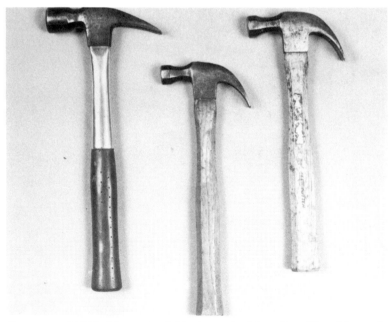

Hammers. LEFT: 20 oz. straight claw, steel handle with rubber grip.
CENTER: 13 oz. curved claw, octagon neck. RIGHT: 16 oz. curved claw,
octagon neck. $15.00-$25.00 each.

Tack hammers. TOP: Magnetic, with logo on top. BOTTOM: Magnetic, with "Keen Kutter" on side. $15.00-$22.00 each.

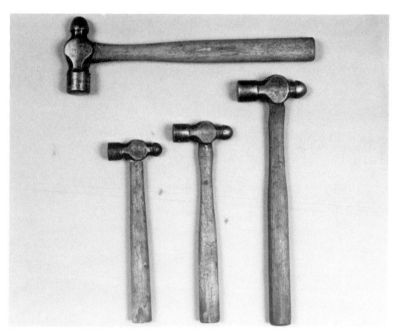

Ballpein hammers, 24 oz., 6 oz., 12 oz., and 16 oz., $20.00-$30.00 each.

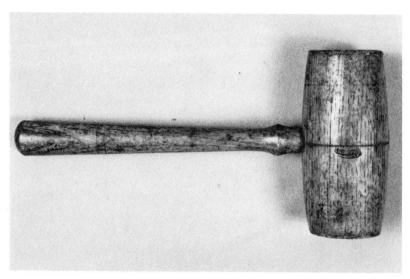

Wooden mallet, has double stamp, $15.00-$20.00.

No. K8 oil stone, in original cardboard box, used for sharpening tools, $25.00-$35.00.

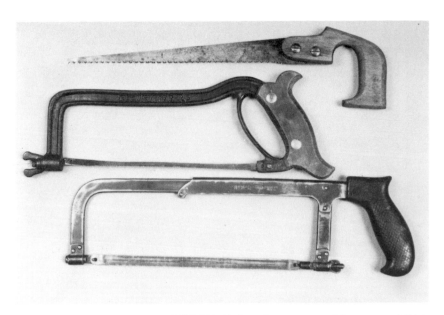

TOP: Keyhole saw, $20.00. CENTER: Dehorning saw, cast iron, wood handle, $30.00. BOTTOM: No. K48 pistol grip hack saw with Keen Kutter hacksaw blade. Hacksaw, $25.00; hacksaw blade, $5.00.

TOP: Adjustable flooring saw, $55.00. CENTER: No. K88 Skewback hand saw with 20″ blade, $35.00. BOTTOM: No. K24 Skewback hand saw with 26″ blade; $35.00. Value is determined by logo on blade.

8" Rip saw blade in original carton, blade is mint, $20.00-$30.00.

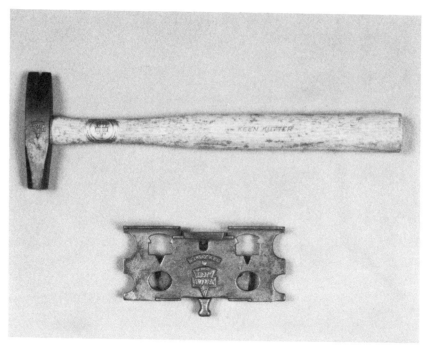

TOP: Saw set hammer, 7 oz., original sticker, hammer was never used, $30.00.
BOTTOM: Saw tool for one or two-man cross cut saw, $15.00-$18.00.

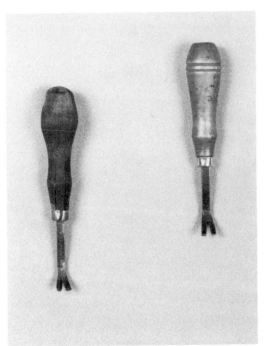

Tack claws, $7.00-$12.00 each.

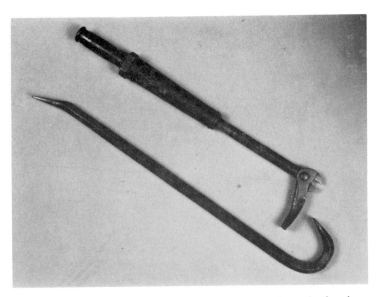

TOP: Nail puller, $25.00-$35.00. BOTTOM: Pinch or ripping bar, $5.00-$15.00.

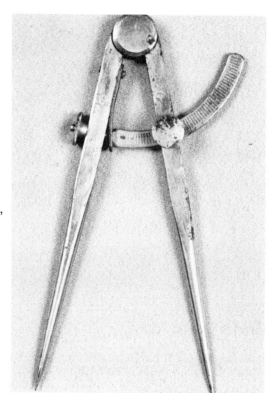

6″ wing or compass dividers, $20.00.

Marking gauge, $20.00-$25.00. Scratch awl with red plastic handle, $8.00.

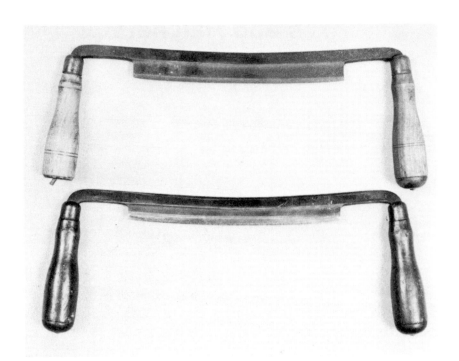

Drawing knives, 8″ blade lengths, top knife has "Keen Kutter" written out; bottom knife has logo. $15.00-$20.00 each.

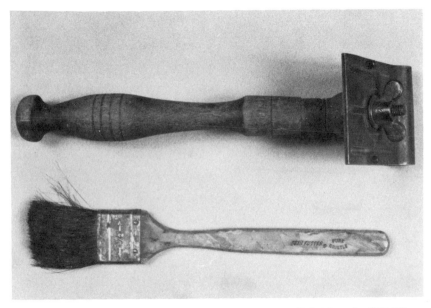

Floor and cabinet scraper, $20.00-$25.00. 1½″ Paint brush, $10.00.

Axes and Hatchets

Broad axe, Shapleigh Day marking, $75.00-$100.00. This broad axe was marketed 1847-1863 by the Shapleigh, Day & Company.

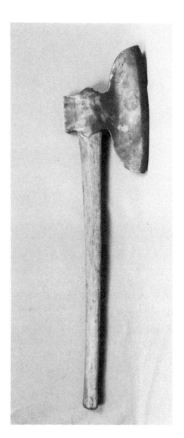

Broad axe, has large logo, $100.00-$125.00.

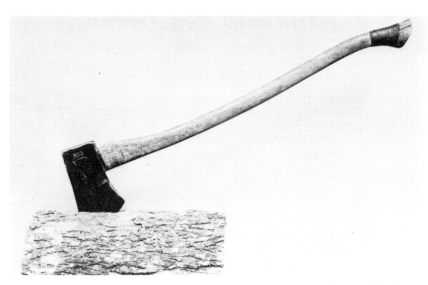

No. 5 single bit axe with special composition pattern, $15.00-$25.00.

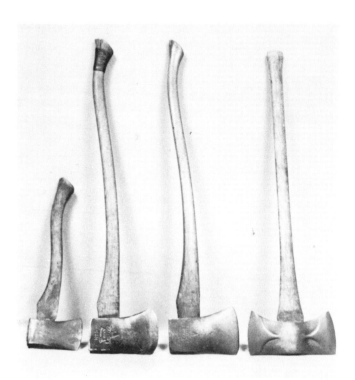

LEFT TO RIGHT: Boy's hand axe; No. 5 single bit; single bit, Michigan pattern; double bit, Western pattern. $15.00-$25.00 each.

TOP: Axe box for single bit axes, $12.00. BOTTOM: Dove tailed axe box for double bit axes, $20.00.

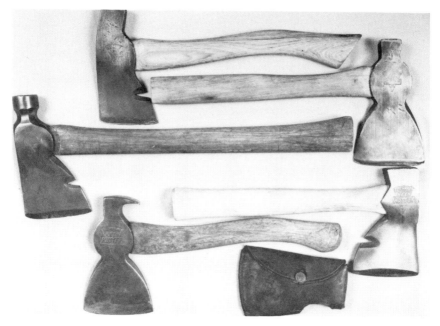

TOP TO BOTTOM: 3¼″ barrel hatchet; 4″ cut shingling hatchet; 3½″ cut rig builders hatchet; 3¾″ flooring hatchet; 4″ claw hatchet; hatchet sheath. $17.00-$32.00 each.

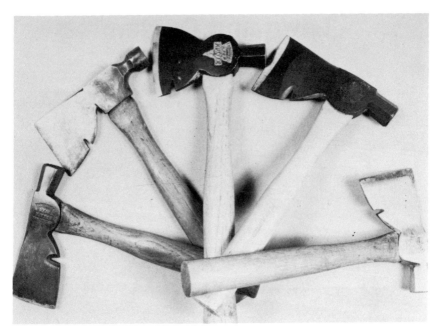

LEFT TO RIGHT: 2½″ cut lathing hatchet; 3¼″ cut half hatchet; 3½″ cut shingling hatchet; half hatchet (mint); 3¼″ half hatchet. $17.00-$32.00 each.

TOP TO BOTTOM: 3¼″ Scout axe; 4″ broad or bench hatchet; 3¼″ house axe; 4½″ broad or bench hatchet; 3¼″ house axe, $17.00-$32.00 each.

Lawn and Garden

Post card advertising Keen Kutter lawn mower. This post card has some of the writing cut off. Post cards, undamaged, $15.00-$25.00.

Back of Keen Kutter post card.

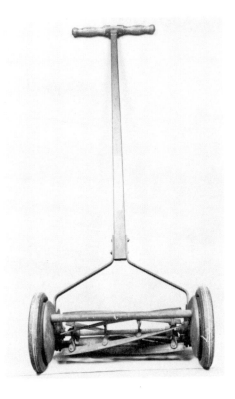

Lawn mower. "Keen Kutter" is on both wheels as well as on handle. Has rubber tires, $25.00.

Gas cans, $10.00-$25.00.

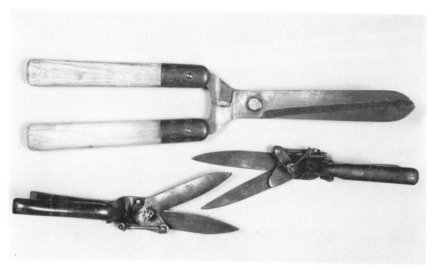

Hedge shears, $10.00-$15.00. Grass shears, $5.00-$10.00.

Horse clippers, $10.00. Garden trowel, $10.00.

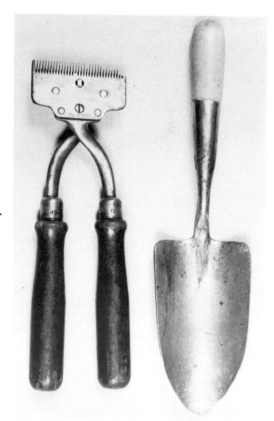

Bush scythe, 18″, mint with paper sticker in right hand corner, $25.00.

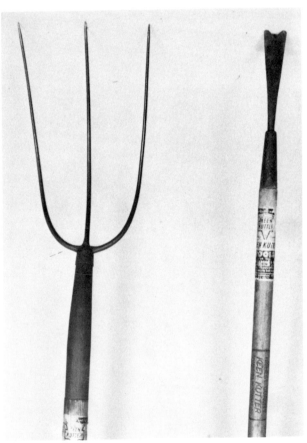

Hay fork, $10.00-$15.00. Dandelion spud or weeder, $10.00-$15.00.

Post hole digger, post hole auger. $10.00-$15.00 each.

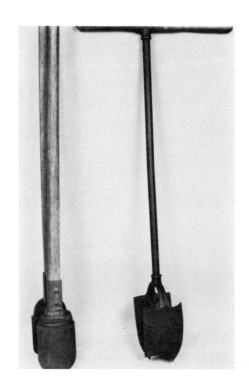

Eye hoes, $10.00-$15.00.

LEFT TO RIGHT: Square point dirt shovel; round point spade; small square point dirt shovel. $10.00-$15.00 each.

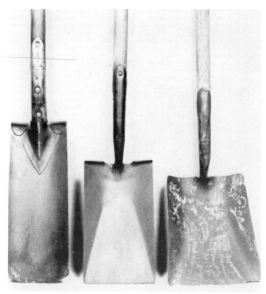

Drain spade, $10.00-$15.00. Square point dirt shovels, $10.00-$15.00 each.

Razors, Shears, and Scissors

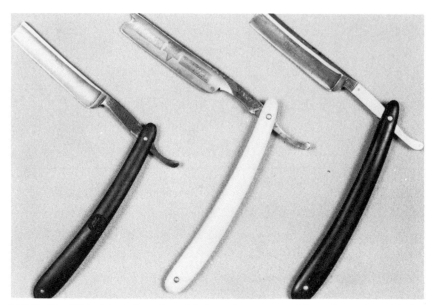

LEFT: No. K15, black handle with logo in center of handle and on blade. CENTER: No. K746, white handle, celluloid, logo etched in gold on blade. RIGHT: No. K128, logo etched in gold on blade plus Mother of Pearl on end of blade. $25.00-$50.00 each.

Razor strops. TOP: No. K94 professional combination, double swing, length 24", width 2½", $30.00-$35.00. BOTTOM: No. K80 combination double swing, 24" length, 2½" width, $25.00.

No. K20 Kombination razor hone (one stone to a tin box), $35.00-$40.00.

No. K15 Razor hone in pasteboard box, $35.00-$40.00.

52

LEFT: Safety razor with metal handle, $10.00-$20.00. RIGHT: Junior safety razor with metal handle, $10.00-$20.00.

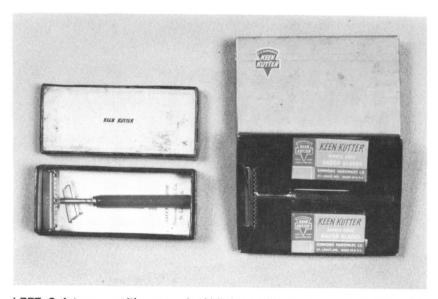

LEFT: Safety razor with one pack of blades and instructions, $10.00-$20.00. RIGHT: Safety razor with each cardboard case containing five blades, $10.00-$20.00.

Various packs of razor blades from early Simmons to Shapleigh, $2.00-$6.00 each.

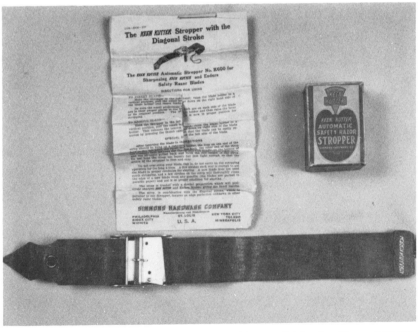

No. K600 safety razor stropper in original box, with instructions, $30.00.

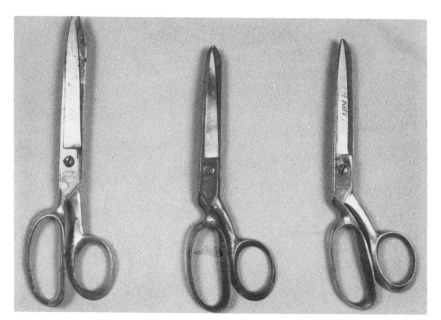

LEFT: 8″ straight trim scissors. CENTER: 7″ bent trimmers. RIGHT: 7″ bent trimmers. $4.00-$8.00 each.

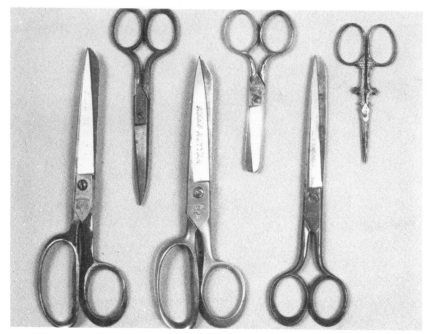

Scissors. TOP ROW, LEFT TO RIGHT: 5½″ ladies; 4″ pocket; lace or embroidery. BOTTOM ROW, LEFT TO RIGHT: 7″ Japan handle; 7″ nickel plated; 7″ ladies. $4.00-$8.00 each.

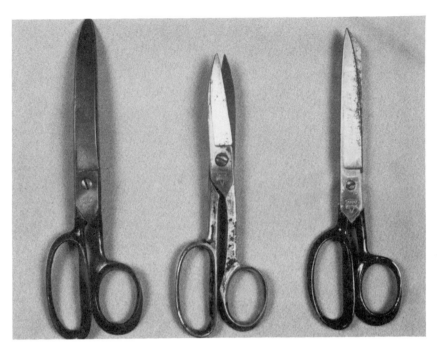

LEFT: 9″ curved blade shears, $6.00-$10.00. CENTER. No. K-11-D Dental snips, $6.00-$10.00. RIGHT: 8″ shears, $4.00-$8.00.

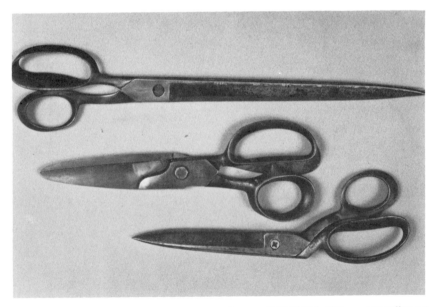

TOP: Paper shears. CENTER: Kitchen shears. BOTTOM: 10″ carpet tailer or upholster shears. $10.00-$15.00 each.

Pocket Knives

Pocket knives. TOP: #882 Barlow pattern, black bone handle. CENTER: No. K254 Barlow pattern, bone handle. LOWER LEFT: No. K2884, ¾ white celluloid handle. LOWER RIGHT: Pruning knife with cocobolo handle. (Knives vary in price according to condition.) $10.00-$30.00 each.

TOP LEFT: No. K18 pearl celluloid handle. TOP RIGHT: No. 886 stage handle. MIDDLE SECTION: Green celluloid handle; bone handle; stag handle; 02235N gold glitter handle. All the above, $10.00-$30.00 each. LOWER LEFT: Never sharpened, still marked on blade, ''0214TK'', red and black glitter celluloid handle, $65.00.

Kitchen

Waffle iron, cast iron, has four sections, each with Keen Kutter logo. Has "E. C. Simmons" embossed on lid. $150.00.

Table cutlery, silver plate, set has six knives and six forks, $55.00.

Apple parer. Pares entire apple and ejects it, patent date May 24, 1898, $50.00.

Kraut cutter, single blade, 9″ x 26½″, patent date October 1904. ''Keen Kutter'' marked on side and on top, $35.00.

Mincing knives for chopping lettuce, celery and other foods for salads, etc., $10.00-$20.00 each. Cookbook, small, comes with food chopper, $15.00.

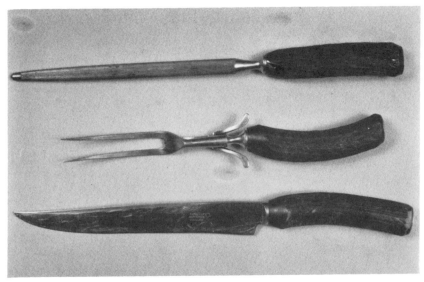

Carving set, 3 piece stag handle. $45.00-$55.00.

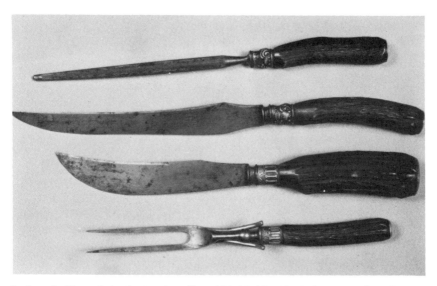

2 piece knife and steel, stag handles, $20.00-$25.00. 2 piece stag handle carving set, $25.00-$35.00.

Box or can openers, $15.00-$20.00.

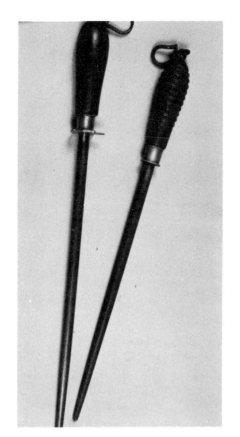

Butcher steel, 14″ with brass logo for guard, $25.00. 12″ Butcher steel, $15.00.

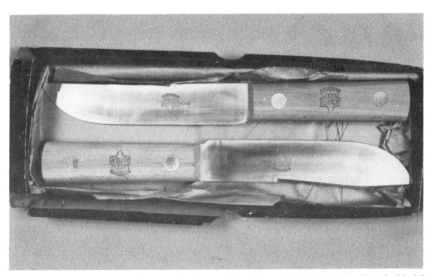

No. K160 6″ butcher knives, mint in original box, $15.00 each. Used, $8.00 each.

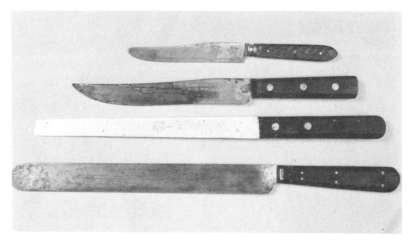

TOP: Kitchen knife. 2nd: Butcher knife. 3rd and BOTTOM: Cake knives. $8.00-$15.00 each.

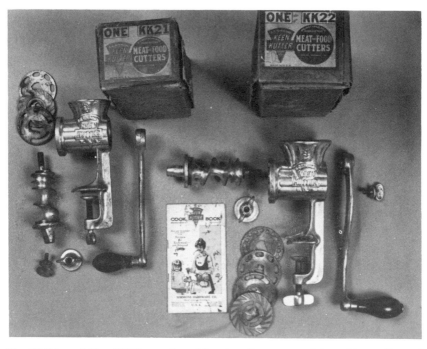

No. KK21 and No. KK22 meat and food cutters, complete with cardboard boxes and cookbooks, $20.00-$25.00 each.

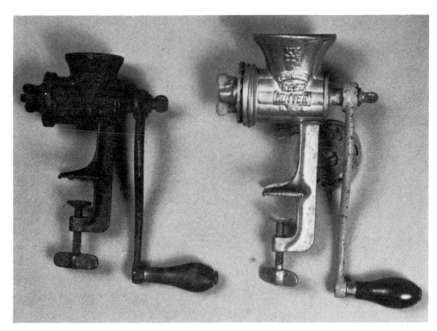

LEFT: No. KK10 food chopper, $7.00. RIGHT: No. KK22½ food chopper with extra cutters, $9.00.

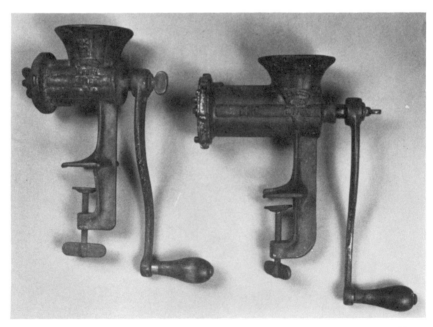

LEFT: No. KK23 food chopper, clamp-to-table model, $7.00. RIGHT: No. K110 meat chopper, clamp-to-table model, $12.00.

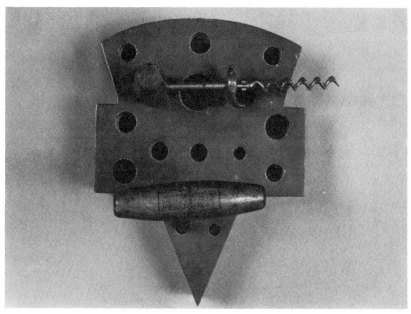

Cork screws, $15.00-$25.00 each. (Top cork screw is a self puller).

Advertisements

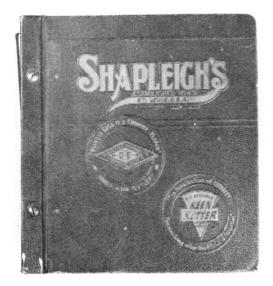

1942 Shapleigh Keen Kutter - Diamond Edge 27 section catalog, 4″ thick, $125.00.

Simmons mail order want books; Shapleigh's want book; 1912 pocket ledger, $20.00-$35.00 each.

Advertisement found in November 7, 1908 *Saturday Evening Post,* $10.00-$15.00.

Name plate, solid brass, came off of a showcase, $50.00.

Advertisement found in November 7, 1908 *Saturday Evening Post,* $10.00-$15.00.

Wooden 6″ x 59″ sign to hang above a display, colors are yellow and red, $20.00-$30.00.

Order By Mail blank, unused, $5.00-$8.00.

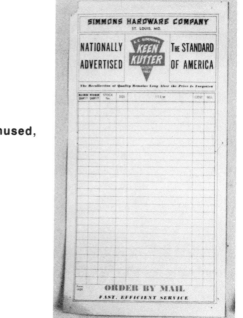

Advertising tin, 9¾″ x 27¾″, signs found on buildings, fences, etc., advertising store name and location carrying Keen Kutter products, $25.00-$30.00.

Fold-up hand fan with logo. The back of this fan is a floral design, $35.00.

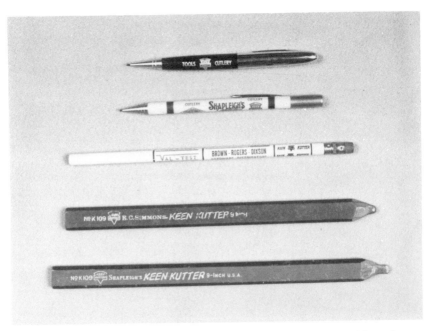

Mechanical pencils, pencil, carpenter pencils, $7.00-$15.00 each.

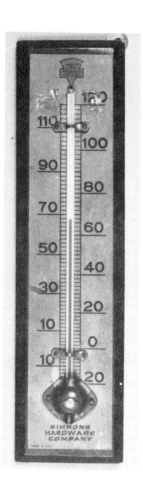

Thermometers, 1¾" x 7½", and 2½" x 9" indoor/outdoor. $30.00-$45.00 each.

Electric clock, 15" x 15", $125.00

Tin wall calendar, pad type, has hardware store name and location, $65.00.

1957 paper calendars with hardware store name and location, $15.00-$20.00 each.

Miscellaneous

Logo design punch and chisel displays, $25.00 each.

Knife display case, four sided, marked on top and on all glasses, $110.00.

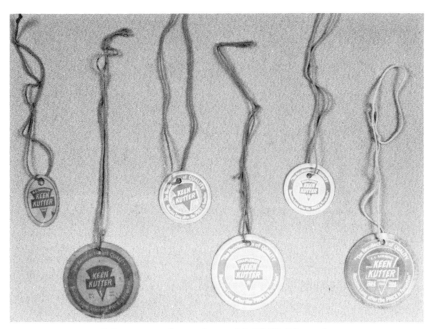

Price tags, tie-on type, $1.00-$2.00 each.

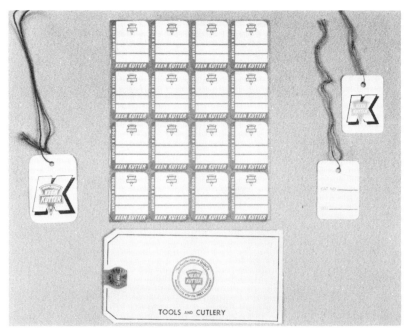

Sheet with sixteen price stickers, $6.00-$10.00. Freight tag, $3.00. Tie on tags, $1.00-$2.00.

Lapel pin, axe design, $30.00-$45.00.

Lapel button with logo, $5.00-$10.00.

Watch fob, pocket strap, $50.00-$75.00.

Wagon, ball bearing wheels, $125.00-$175.00.

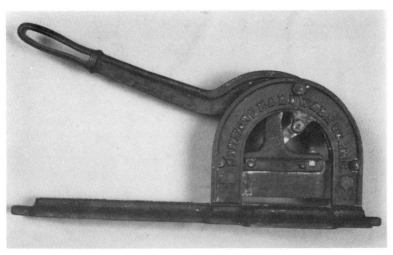

Tobacco cutter, base marked "E. C. Simmons, Keen Kutter, St. Louis USA", $175.00.

Trunk locks, $40.00-$50.00.

Padlocks, $75.00-$100.00.

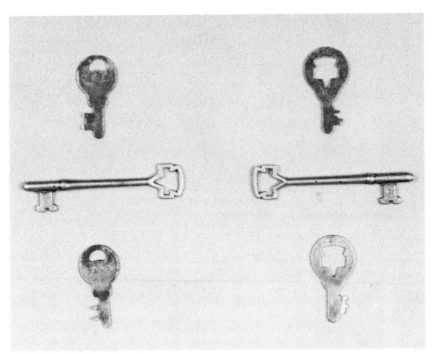

Padlock keys, $10.00-$15.00 each. Skeleton keys, $10.00 each.

Oil bottles, $15.00-$20.00 each.

Leather gun holster, $25.00.

Flashlight, two-cell, $25.00.

Other popularly priced illustrated value guides from COLLECTOR BOOKS

Barbie Dolls by Paris, Susan & Carol Manos, 5½ x 8½, 80 pages, paperbound, $5.95.

The Basket Book by Don & Carol Raycraft, 5½ x 8½, 80 pages, paperbound, $5.95.

Black Glass by Margaret James, 5½ x 8½, 80 pages, paperbound, $5.95.

Coffee Mills by Terry Friend, 5½ x 8½, 80 pages, paperbound, $5.95.

Collectible Salt and Pepper Shakers by Helene Guarnaccia, 5½ x 8½, 80 pages, paperbound, $5.95.

Decorated Country Stoneware by Don & Carol Raycraft, 5½ x 8½, 80 pages, paperbound, $5.95.

Metal Molds by Eleanore Bunn, 5½ x 8½, 80 pages, paperbound, $5.95.

The Oak Book by Jane Fryberger, 5½ x 8½, 80 pages, paperbound, $5.95.

Police Relics by George Virgines, 5½ x 8½, 80 pages, paperbound, $5.95.

Sea Shells by Carol Glassmire, 5½ x 8½, 80 pages, paperbound, $5.95.

Trolls by Susan Miller, 5½ x 8½, 80 pages, paperbound, $5.95.

The Wicker Book by Jane Fryberger, 5½ x 8½, 80 pages, paperbound, $5.95.

Order from your favorite bookstore or

COLLECTOR BOOKS
P.O. Box 3009
Paducah, Kentucky 42001

When ordering, please add $1.00 for postage and handling.

Write for free listing of all other COLLECTOR BOOKS titles.